For Kirk, Claire, and anyone with a dream to be the owner.

Buying vs. Starting a Small Business: Search or Startup?
A guide to keep you from going broke.

5-Star Reviews for *Buying vs. Starting a Small Business*

*****

"Buying vs Starting a Small Business offers a welcoming tone that simplifies complex concepts. Its examples and ideas are accessible to novices, ensuring clarity without unnecessary complexity, all conveyed succinctly."

Ted J Leverette, The original *Business Buyer Advocate*®
PartnerOnCall.com

*****

"This book is a great example of why I love David's content so much. He cuts through the fluff that defines so much content in this topic area and focuses on the core issues impacting aspiring business owners. Strongly recommend this quick and easy read for anyone considering buying or starting a business."

Mike Finger, 4X Exit Entrepreneur & Small Business Coach
ExitOasis.com

*****

"I've always appreciated David's honesty about being an entrepreneur, and this book is no exception. The candid insights shared throughout the pages offer a refreshing perspective that both aspiring and seasoned entrepreneurs can benefit from. As someone who values practicality, I found the book to be particularly useful. It provides concrete, actionable advice on buying and starting a business, which is essential for anyone looking to embark on this journey."

Mylène Roy, Project Co-Ordinator, Small Business Education
ProfitLearn.com

*****

"Buying vs. Starting a Small Business: Search or Startup? Is a great book written by a person that lives and breathes business. I really appreciate Dave's perspective because he looks at every angle and focuses on the areas people miss or overlook in the process. I highly recommend this book to anyone looking to start their own business."

Giuseppe Grammatico, Franchise Consultant & Host
The Franchise Freedom Podcast

*****

"I just finished reading this book. It was a simple and easy read that kept my attention throughout. It's a great guide for anyone weighing the decision between buying an existing business or starting a new one, offering clear, practical advice and honest insights about the risks and challenges. Great read!"

Nunzio Presta, Tech Entrepreneur & President
BuyAndSellaBusiness.com

*****

"Like David, I help small business owners become highly profitable and fulfilled in their work and I've served thousands in this capacity as an accountant and money coach. I wish all my clients had the financial foundation and perspectives shared in this book. David's approach to analyzing a business idea is radically honest and simple. "

Katherine Pomerantz, Money Storyteller
KatherinePomerantz.com

*****

"As a Business school professor, I read a lot of books that claim to help people who are on their entrepreneurship journey. Most are highly theoretical, or worse unrealistic "entrepreneurship porn". David's book "Buying vs. Starting a Small Business: Search or Startup, A Guide..." is the real deal. A well organized, step-by-step guide that leads you through a series of "lessons". Each of the chapters is a concise well illustrated summary of each chapter's lesson. The book is brief, without being cursory. The pros and cons of each option are fairly laid out and explained in understandable language with enough real-world examples so that the reader gains an overview of the topic. If you are considering where your entrepreneurship journey will take you next. If you should be a Buyer or a Starter, an evening spent reading this book will be a real help as you think through the process. Highly Recommend!"

Kevin Rogers, Professor- Sales, Marketing & Entrepreneurship
Oulton College

*****

"Buying vs. Starting a Small Business" by David C Barnett is a timely and insightful guide for aspiring entrepreneurs. Barnett skillfully breaks down the complex decision-making process into easy-to-follow steps, making it feel like a mini-course in book form. His clear and practical advice helps readers navigate the choice between buying an existing business and starting a new one, ensuring they can make well-informed decisions."

Peter Lount, Wealth Advisor
ReturnOnLife.ca

Why invest your time and money into this book:

If the reviews aren't enough, let me tell you what to expect if you take the time to read this book.

1. You'll learn to appreciate the real risks of being a business owner.
2. You'll be better able to assess whether your business or acquisition target makes sense for the likely outcomes.
3. You'll learn to ground your dreams in the awful confines of actual, measurable reality.
4. You'll learn to identify and inoculate yourself against the mindset risks of consuming *entrepreneur success porn*.

It's hard to learn the skills of entrepreneurship from a book.

Success in this arena is about understanding what you control, the likelihood of success and having the courage to adapt and pivot your trajectory while you're already underway.

If you've never been in business before, that might seem difficult to consider.

Throughout this book, I'll give you examples of how to use innovative and resourceful thinking to re-imagine your business ideas in ways that reduce the investment, reduce the risk and grow the potential for returns.

Here's the big secret—Entrepreneurs everywhere are trying to maximize their profits while minimizing investment and risk.

But—new people to the game often don't. They don't even consider this and so they end up making huge investments and taking on big debts even if there is insufficient upside potential.

If you're worried that this might be you, read this book.

Contact and Learning co-ordinates: David Barnett can be reached via e-mail at info@alpatlantic.com. Please put 'Buying vs Starting a Business' in the subject line along with the subject of your e-mail.

David Barnett's YouTube channel is https://www.SmallBusinessAndDealMakingPodcast.com where questions are discussed regarding buying, selling, managing and financing small and medium sized businesses.

You can follow the audio with any of the major podcast services by searching for 'David C Barnett Small Business.'

Come to my blog anytime to find articles, videos, online courses, books and information on my consulting services. The site is https://www.DavidCBarnett.com

I regularly give seminars and presentations on the topics of local investing, buying small businesses and preparing to sell small businesses. I welcome the opportunity to discuss a speaking engagement or appearance. Simply reach out to me and my team at info@alpatlantic.com

Want to call and chat about a deal? Quick phone consultations can be arranged at https://www.CallDavidBarnett.com

Receive my regular, informative e-mails by clicking here:
https://www.DavidCBarnettList.com
Easy unsubscribe should you ever choose because I use MailChimp.

David C Barnett Product Map

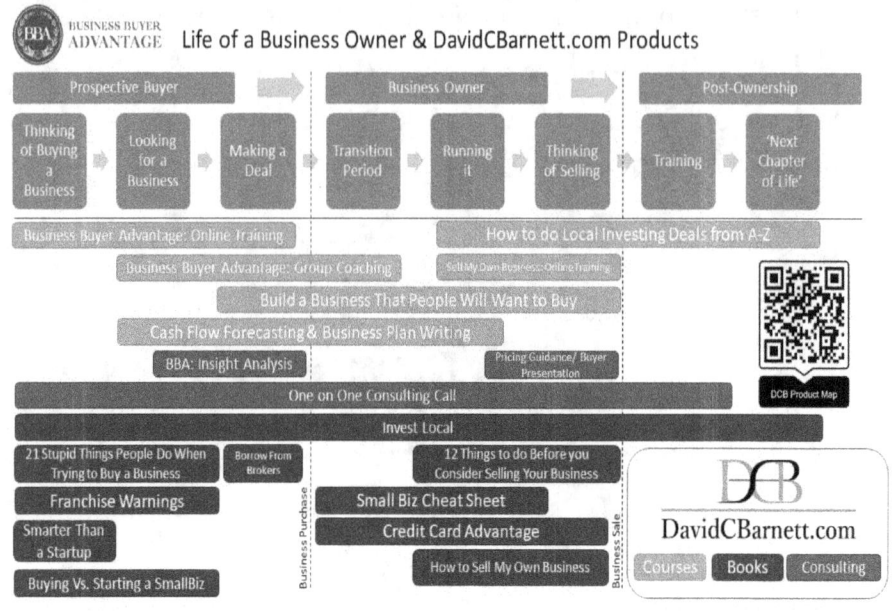

For a complete rundown of my courses, services and books, with an introduction video, check out the David C Barnett Product Map here: https://dbarnett.gumroad.com/l/DCBProductMap/free

A GUIDE TO KEEP YOU FROM
GOING BROKE

BUYING VS STARTING A SMALL BUSINESS

DAVID C BARNETT

©2024 By David C Barnett. All Rights Reserved. The material in this book is protected by copyright laws and treaties worldwide. Any unauthorized reprint or use of this material is prohibited. No part of this book may be reproduced or transmitted in any form or by any means, electronic or mechanical, including photocopying, recording, or by an information storage and retrieval system without the express written permission of David C. Barnett.

If you would like to give a copy of this book to someone, please send them to get a legitimate copy.

https://www.DavidCBarnett.com or Amazon stores worldwide.

***

David C Barnett and his team provide the following services to small business buyers/sellers and entrepreneurs:

1. Consulting to help you buy or sell.
2. Online courses for self-serve education.
3. Books.
4. Evaluation services for businesses and Machinery/Equipment.
5. Live event teaching and workshops both in-person and virtual.

For more information, visit the sections at the end of this book.

Contact David and his team:

Email: info@alpatlantic.com

Main Office Line: 1 (833) 935-2688

Web: https://www.DavidCBarnett.com choose 'Work with David.'

Contents

- About the Author 12
- Introduction, who is David? 16
- Motivation 19
- Success in Business vs. Not Closing. 23
- Measure your Resources 27
- The Race to Breakeven. 32
- Investors vs. Entrepreneurs... 38
- Hedging Entrepreneurial Risk 42
- Using Debt 48
- Creativity and Resourcefulness 56
- Valuing Businesses 63
- Finding a Business to Buy 69
- Buying a Platform Business to Launch your Idea............... 74
- The Biggest Risk in Buying a Small Business 78
- Conclusion 83
- Additional Works by the Author... 86
- Live Workshops and Seminars.. 118

About the Author

Welcome to my program on learning the differences, risks, pitfalls and benefits/costs of Buying vs. Starting a Business.

Business has always been an interest of mine and I pursued many childhood enterprises. When I finished high school, I attended Bishop's University in Lennoxville, Quebec, to study business administration. When I got out of university, I started a business with a friend. It only lasted a few months but helped me secure a position in advertising sales with a Yellow Pages publisher.

The Yellow Pages was my first chance to get an X-ray view into the realities of small business.

After six years in advertising sales, I started investing in real estate. I bought a house and eventually added two triplexes and a four-unit property. I started another company with a partner and eventually sold it 18 months later. We did junk removal, and it was a lot of fun.

In 2006 I started another new company. Advantage Liquidity Partners Ltd. was a broker of commercial debt and finance solutions. The company helped businesses get commercial mortgages, capital and operating leases, factoring facilities (the sale of accounts receivable), bank loans under government guarantee programs and revolving credit facilities. I had taken a two-day course from a California firm on how to professionally assemble a loan or lease package and figured I could learn the rest along the way.

I started to learn from the companies that I used to fund loans and took a chance to do some of my own deals with my own money. This was the inspiration for my first book; *Invest Local*. In the fall of 2008, during the Wall St. financial crisis, over half of the lenders I used to fund my 'B' deals went out of business. My whole deal pipeline shriveled up and I began to look again for opportunity.

While doing financing for small businesses I had run into several people trying to finance business acquisitions. I found that the business brokerage market in my area was largely under-served and that this might be a place for me. I joined a national franchise business brokerage and bought the local office in 2009. It was also around this time that I became a Certified Machinery & Equipment Appraiser.

Business brokerage is one of the most exciting things I have ever done. I miss it almost every day. It combines the financial deal making of commercial real estate with the emotions of home sales. It requires someone who can educate a client and teach them how to buy or sell a business. It also has the worst cash flow characteristics of any business I know, and I don't recommend it to anyone, especially someone like me who had two small children at the time.

While I was a business broker, I sold over 35 businesses. By any account, I was the most successful business broker ever in my area. I also did two nine-month stretches with no deal closings, meaning no revenue, and also went through a 14-month period with no bank involvement in any deals. This means that while I did get paid, it largely came in the form of payments over time. To say the least, I can be creative to get something done.

Some of those experiences inspired another book I've written, *How to Borrow Money from your Business Broker*.

My last big deal as a broker was selling a fried chicken franchise. It was also one of my first listings three years earlier. Yes - I did 36 months of work before getting paid. Because of this inconsistent cash flow, I decided to get out of business brokerage at the end of 2011.

I now work along with my small team as an advisor and consultant to people buying and selling small businesses and people trying to obtain business financing.

I also manage my own portfolio of private finance deals and write books.

This is my eighth book. I've also written *How to Sell My Own Business, Invest Local, Credit Card Advantage, 21 Stupid Things People do When Trying to Buy a Business, 12 Things to do Before you Consider Selling Your Business, Smarter Than a Startup* and *Franchise Warnings*. I've also created a few FREE giveaways that you can also learn about at the back of this book.

My books are available from Amazon as Kindle, Audiobooks and some are available as paperbacks. You can get pdf versions on my website, https://www.DavidCBarnett.com.

I've also developed online courses to teach people how to buy or sell small businesses, develop business systems, build financial forecasts and business plans and how to do their own local investing deals.

Now, without further delay, let's discuss this hot topic of buying vs. starting a business.

Thank You,

Introduction, who is David?

Welcome to *Buying vs. Starting a Small Business*!

Lesson #1. Introducing David.

Hello, my name is David C Barnett. I've been an entrepreneur my whole life.

I even spent a few years in business school because I thought it would make me a better businessman, only to discover that they were trying to turn me into what I now call a *Fortune 500 bureaucrat*.

Currently, I'm a single dad of two amazing teens and I live on Canada's rugged East Coast, near the Bay of Fundy.

If we just talk about my business endeavors as an adult, I've owned and operated five different real businesses.

What make a business 'real' in my mind?

I was able to pay myself the same wage or more than what I would have earned working for someone else.

This is important and we'll be talking about this more later on.

One of these five businesses was a business that I bought from another entrepreneur.

It happened to be a business brokerage firm.

Business brokers are to businesses like realtors are to houses. It was a professional office that helped people buy and sell small businesses and it put me in the path of a lot of entrepreneurs and business owners. It also allowed me to meet many people who wanted to own one.

Over the course of three years, I handled the transition of over 35 businesses from one owner to another.

The experience running that business brokerage led me to the world of consulting, writing books and educating people online.

Since that time, I've worked with hundreds of prospective business buyers and sellers to either help them complete a deal or know when not to.

My client list has grown to include businesspeople in English-speaking countries all around the world.

I've helped thousands of people learn more about buying, selling, financing, and managing small and medium sized businesses through the books I've written and the YouTube channel I maintain.

I set up a direct URL to the YouTube channel if you want to check it out. It's at https://www.SmallBusinessAndDealMakingPodcast.com

I've worked with hundreds of students though my online courses and group coaching programs aimed at helping people make educated and risk-reduced deals to buy businesses which will provide for their families and increase the quality of their lifestyles.

Now, what happened to those five businesses of mine that I told you about?

Well, two were sold, two were closed because they stopped working well enough and one is still working today.

In this course, I'm going to be exploring the differences between buying an existing business versus starting a new one.

I'm going to be challenging some of the widely held beliefs that exist out there about business success rates and about what kinds of investment go into becoming a business owner.

There is a lot of content in this program. There will be many new ideas for most of you.

Now, let's start with uncovering the 'why' behind your entrepreneurial impulse.

Motivation

Lesson #2, Understanding your motivations.

Why do you want to be in business?

I ask this question all the time.

I hear many fantastic responses, let me share a few with you:

- I want to earn more money.
- I want to have more control over my life.
- I want to work less.
- I want to move into semi-retirement.
- I don't have any opportunities to work in my field.
- I can't find a job and need an income.
- I've reached the limit of advancement with my present employer.
- I want to move to a smaller town or back to be close to my family.

It goes on and on and it's completely subjective to each person.

When you have a job, someone else is stressing out about all the details that make sure the money is in the bank when you try to cash your paycheque.

If your employer closes, you often have access to government unemployment benefits of some kind.

Governments of the world have done much to watch out for the interests of employees.

Even when businesses fail and end up in liquidation, unpaid wages are usually paid out ahead of things like bank loans.

When you move to the world of entrepreneurship and self-employment, you can no longer look to the state to offer you support when things get bad.

You have to be truly self-reliant.

This can be daunting, especially for those in America who may also lose access to health care benefits when they leave a job.

There are a lot of celebrity business boosters out there who talk constantly about how you need to be dedicated and motivated to make things happen in your own business.

They're right, but dedication, motivation and effort are not enough.

You also need to be competent and *not make mistakes*.

If you do make mistakes, you need to have the resources to survive and make it long enough to recover.

Sometimes you can avoid mistakes and still end up in a crisis.

Just look at what the Covid-19 pandemic did to many small businesses out there.

Many have failed because they were not able to adapt or adapt quickly enough to new ways of serving customers to keep moving forward.

Now, there is also a downside to dedication.

It is possible to be so dedicated to making a business succeed that it consumes you and all your resources.

I've seen people get trapped by this phenomenon.

They identify with their business so much, and they feel that if the business fails, that makes them a failure as well.

Part of this is cultural, some societies are more forgiving than others when it comes to business closures.

Here's what I'd like you to do.

I want you to write out a goal about your business.

It has to include what you want from your business and what you're willing to give to make it happen.

For example: *I will own a business that will pay me a salary of $90,000 each year. This business will let me achieve a greater work/life balance by limiting my work to 50 hours per week. I can do this business from home so I won't have to commute, and I can move to a smaller community which is more affordable. I'm willing to invest $20,000 of my savings, borrow $30,000 from the bank and work hard for the next year to achieve this level of success.*

Not only does this format of goal help you set your sights on what you want, but it clearly defines what you're willing to give to achieve it.

It draws a line in the sand.

In this example, if you invest the time, money and incur the debts but still haven't achieved the business you wanted, you know it's time to quit or seriously review your plan.

But don't feel so bad, as we move along, I'm going to show you different ways to reduce the risks that come with being in business.

In the next lesson, we're going to dive more deeply into the idea of what makes a business successful or not.

Key Themes (Lessons)

1. Understanding Personal Motivation: Identifying and understanding your unique reasons for wanting to start a business.
2. Self-Reliance in Entrepreneurship: Recognizing the shift from job security to self-reliance and the implications this has on your personal and financial stability.
3. Balanced Dedication and Goal Setting: Setting realistic business goals that balance dedication with personal well-being and clearly define what you're willing to invest and expect in return.

Key Questions for You to Seriously Answer:

1. Personal Motivation: Why do you want to start your own business, and how do your reasons align with your personal goals and values?
2. Self-Reliance: How prepared are you to handle the responsibilities and uncertainties that come with being self-reliant in your business?
3. Financial Stability: What is your plan for managing financial instability or unexpected crises that may arise in your business?
4. Work-Life Balance: How will you ensure that your dedication to your business does not consume all your resources or negatively impact your personal life?
5. Goal Setting and Evaluation: What specific goals do you have for your business, and what criteria will you use to evaluate your progress and success?

Success in Business vs. Not Closing.

Lesson #3 Success in business vs. simply not closing.

We've all heard the stats... A huge number of small businesses fail within the first five years after starting.

While understanding how risky business can be is important, I want to focus on those that don't close.

Some of those are also not successful.

What do I mean?

Well, simply not closing is hardly a sign of success.

I work with small businesses all the time and I see their financial statements.

There are many businesses out there, some that have been open for years, that don't make any money.

Worse still, some don't even pay their owners for their time OR make any profits.

Is this a <u>successful</u> business?

Let's consider the experience of some real business experts... the researchers over at Harvard University.

In 2012, Harvard released a study of venture-backed firms that raised at least $1 million dollars.

These are business startups which are put together so that wealthy investors can put in money in the hopes of earning a rate of return after all the expenses and employees have been paid.

It's also important to note that these investors believe that these businesses have potential, otherwise they'd be investing in other, less risky things.

That's a high hurdle, but these people are pros, and know what they're doing, right?

The result of the study was startling.

Of the 2000 businesses that the researchers looked at, 22.5% failed after 6 years... If you consider failure to be their closure and liquidation. However, what is really telling is that 1500 of the businesses failed to deliver any return to the investors.

If your goal is to simply not close, then these businesses did well compared to the usual dire statistics that we often see about small business failure rates.

But if your idea of success is like mine, then it means that succeeding in business is much harder than even those pessimistic business failure stats tell us.

My idea of success goes like this:

1. A business should be able to pay all its bills,
2. Pay the owner a fair market wage for the work they do daily in the business.
3. The business also needs to have a surplus of cash such that it can pay its debt service AND give the owner a dividend or rate of return on the cash invested to get things going.

That's a pretty high hurdle, isn't it?

Actually, I don't think so.

You see, if you didn't get into business and instead went out and found a job, you'd be paid a fair market wage for your time.

You could then invest your savings in some kind of investment that would pay you a rate of return.

Even at a low interest rate, putting cash in a savings account would be an improvement over those businesses we just discussed.

In the Harvard study, only 25% of businesses gave any kind of payment back to the investors, let alone returning the principal invested along with investment gains.

I've presented this lesson on risk not because I want to scare you off, but rather because I want to properly calibrate your ambition.

If you go into business, you need to be properly compensated.

If there is any doubt that you will be, then the rewards must be great enough to warrant the risks.

You don't want to be someone who risks time, money, and debt with little hope of great rewards even if the market embraces your new venture.

In the next lesson, we're going to discuss the resources you'll need to get into business whether via starting something new or buying a business that is already running.

www.EasySmallBizSystems.com

Key Themes (Lessons)

1. Defining Business Success: Distinguishing between merely staying open and genuinely succeeding in business.
2. Financial Viability: Emphasizing the importance of a business being able to pay its bills, compensate its owner fairly, and generate a profit.
3. Realistic Expectations and Risk Assessment: Understanding the high risk of failure and the importance of setting realistic expectations for business success.

Key Questions for You to Seriously Answer

1. Definition of Success: What does success mean to you in the context of your business? Is it just staying open, or are you aiming for profitability and growth?
2. Financial Health: How will you ensure your business can pay all its bills, including a fair wage to yourself as the owner?
3. Profitability: What is your plan for ensuring your business not only survives but also generates a profit and provides a return on investment?
4. Risk vs. Reward: Are the potential rewards of your business venture sufficient to justify the risks involved? How have you assessed these risks?
5. Realistic Planning: How will you calibrate your ambitions to align with the realistic challenges and risks of running a business?

Measure your Resources

Lesson #4 Measure your resources and know what you have to work with.

If you're going to go into business for yourself, whether by doing a startup or an acquisition, you need to know what you have to work with.

People often think of this in terms of money.

But there are a great many more resources out there that can be used in some way to help you get what you need to be in business.

Resources can be money, in-kind assets such as a vehicle or space in your home that can be used for the business, and credit- access to the ability to create debts which can be used to buy more assets or cover expenses.

Be creative and thorough.

Education can be an asset, and not just formal education.

You can develop intellectual property that can be monetized in a business simply by investing your time.

Let me give you a few examples.

#1. My experience in business brokerage and entrepreneurship has allowed me to create this program. Once recorded and written, it becomes a source of revenue for me on an ongoing basis, hopefully.

#2. A good friend of mine in Montreal is a fan of street art, both murals and sculpture installations. She created a dossier on many of the artists whose work is on public streets and monetizes this by offering walking tours of street art for tourists.

Nobody must give either me or my Montreal friend 'permission' to monetize our knowledge. We just put it out there for the market to judge. That judgement will present itself in the form of sales revenue or the absence of sales revenue.

The key to understanding what you have available is being creative and resourceful.

Now, what about the people you know?

Do you know someone with underused assets that you could employ in a business?

Maybe a friend has space, machinery, equipment, or other resources that you could potentially use.

I have borrowed a meeting room from a friend with office space on more than one occasion to host small business training seminars for example.

Once your list of resources is complete, you should be able to group them into several categories:

- Cash
- Credit
- Equipment, vehicles, tools
- Spaces, places
- Specific education, knowledge, or skills
- Etc.

Sometimes, creating your list of resources can inspire you with ideas of what kind of new business to create.

Now, what happens if you spend all your money and end up with debts and no profits.

This is important to know.

It's called the **worst-case** scenario.

Back when I bought the business brokerage, my then-wife thought it was risky.

Don't worry, I said, if it doesn't work out, I'll just get a job.

Three years later, I was working for a bank and getting a regular paycheque again.

Understanding your worst-case scenario is fundamental to controlling the fear that normally comes with any great change in life.

As humans, we are wired to fear change for change could lead to death for our ancient ancestors.

With a worst-case scenario in mind, we now have to consider the cost of a pivot.

What will it take in order to achieve this 'plan B.' that we imagine?

In my case, I knew that I was highly skilled and employable, but it can sometimes be hard to find the right job and with no unemployment benefits, how would I live after closing my business?

In my case it came down to a $15,000 emergency fund.

When I got into business, I set aside $15,000 in a different bank from my normal affairs.

This money was to pay for life while I found a job if my business ever failed.

Do you feel that $15,000 is a lot of money to set aside?

You perhaps don't have this kind of cash?

This figure was based on my monthly expenses at the time, and we will be discussing it further as we move along.

So, what are the maximum resources that you have available?

It's whatever you have access to that you're willing to risk, minus some security amount to finance your pivot if things don't work out.

We already know the failure rate of small businesses is high, not acting accordingly would simply be foolish.

Again, as we move forward, I'm going to be sharing even more ways that you can reduce risk on your path to business ownership.

In the next lesson, we're going to discuss the timelines of achieving our goal.

Key Themes (Lessons)

1. Comprehensive Resource Assessment: Understanding and identifying all types of resources available for starting a business, including money, in-kind assets, credit, education, and intellectual property.
2. Creativity and Resourcefulness: Utilizing creativity to identify and leverage non-traditional resources, such as skills, knowledge, and connections.
3. Planning for the Worst-Case Scenario: Recognizing the importance of preparing for potential business failure by setting aside resources for a backup plan.

Key Questions for You to Seriously Answer

1. Resource Inventory: What resources do you have available to start your business? Consider cash, credit, equipment, space, education, skills, and connections.
2. Creative Resource Utilization: How can you creatively leverage your non-monetary resources, such as skills, knowledge, or connections, to support your business venture?
3. Network and Support: Who in your network has underused assets or resources that you might be able to utilize for your business? How can you approach them for support?
4. Worst-Case Scenario Planning: What is your worst-case scenario if your business does not succeed? How can you prepare for this situation?
5. Emergency Fund: How much money do you need to set aside as an emergency fund to support yourself if your business fails, and how will you accumulate this amount?

The Race to Breakeven.

Lesson #5 The race to the breakeven point.

In the previous lesson, we discussed the resources you need in order to get a business off the ground AND we thought about the 'what ifs' of getting involved in something that is by nature very risky.

I want to take some time to discuss the idea of the breakeven point.

If you've ever studied starting a business, you'll remember a chart with lines for expenses and revenues.

Along the vertical axis of the chart are dollars.

Along the horizontal is time, sometimes expressed in months.

As you look from left to right, the lines take off and move through the future.

The sales line starts at zero and begins to move up as it moves to the right.

This represents the increasing sales month after month, hopefully, that your new business will achieve.

The other line represents the expenses.

Unfortunately, it doesn't start at zero.

It usually starts at some higher point.

Why? Most businesses have fixed expenses that need to be paid whether or not we serve a customer.

This is called the overhead.

But there's more.

Most businesses have direct costs. In accounting terms, this is the *cost of sales* or *the cost of goods sold*.

It's the cost of actually delivering the product or service to the customer.

This means that the expense line starts off higher than zero and also continues to grow as you make sales because of these direct costs.

So, ideally, the sales line has a steeper slope than the expense line.

This means, hopefully, that the lines will meet at some point.

The sales line will cross over the expense line meaning that for the first time, you'll make money on each sale.

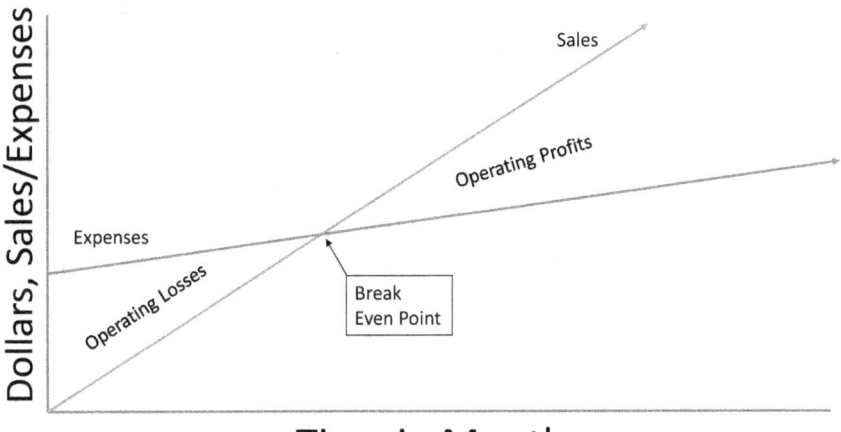

There are a lot of problems with this.

Firstly, we're talking about accounting expenses.

Remember those direct costs? What if you have to invest a lot of money to build an inventory before you make your first sale?

The cash flow consequences of your inventory actually make this race to the breakeven point even more risky than the breakeven analysis would show.

So, not only does the startup entrepreneur have to worry about the investments in machinery, equipment, inventory and expenses like advertising, and that pivot reserve fund, we need something else.

A pot of money to cover losses until we reach the breakeven point!

AND we can never be sure <u>when exactly that will be.</u>

Some businesses take years to hit breakeven.

Even the most carefully crafted business plan is still built upon guesses and assumptions.

How do some entrepreneurs deal with financing these losses before hitting the breakeven point?

Lots of ways:

- They spend money they have saved up.
- They get into debt.
- Or- They don't take a salary and live off the income of a spouse or partner.

If you've ever heard of businesspeople talking about a 'burn rate' for a new business, this is what they're describing.

The burn rate tells us how long we have to live before we're out of cash and credit and have to close the doors.

Many of the young businesses that you see close never reach this breakeven point or they reach the mirage of a breakeven.

The mirage is lying to yourself. For example, staying open and paying the bills while the owner works full time for no pay.

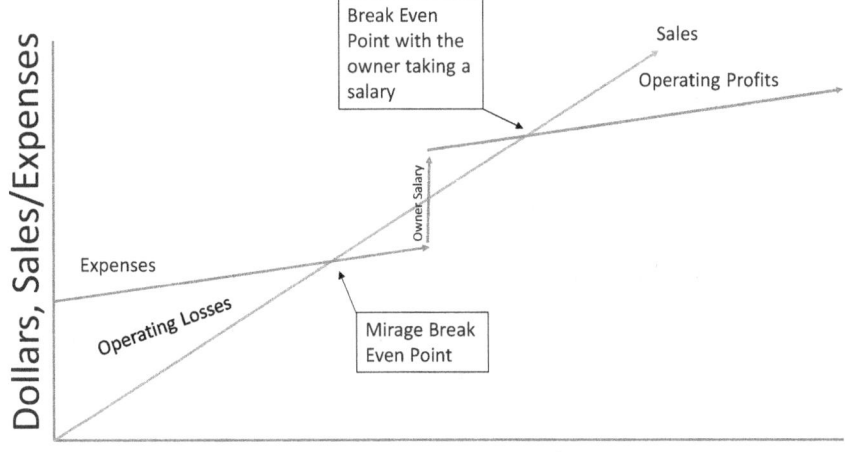

Working full time for no pay is not being successful in business.

If you want to do a really fantastic job of creating a cash flow forecast for a business along with a business plan, you should check out my program on this topic at https://www.BizPlanSchool.com. It's received tons of great feedback, even from people with advanced business degrees who said that I helped simplify a lot of the concepts that they struggled with in school.

There are ways to mitigate this danger, however.

Usually, it's through pre-selling.

For example, signing a contract to provide services before you build your business.

It can be tricky to pull off, but if you're a veteran of an industry with lots of connections who believe in you, they may be willing to be your customer before you can deliver.

Remember before when we discussed resources?

Industry contacts would be a great resource to include on your list.

I hope I haven't turned you off from your entrepreneurial dream, as we move forward, the stories and opportunities will get better, I promise.

Next up we're going to discuss the mindset of getting into business ownership.

There are very different points of view when it comes to being the boss.

https://www.BizPlanSchool.com

Key Themes (Lessons)

1. Understanding the Breakeven Point: Recognizing the importance of reaching the breakeven point, where revenues equal expenses, and the complexities involved in achieving it.
2. Financial Planning and Cash Flow Management: Highlighting the need for careful financial planning, including covering losses until breakeven and understanding the burn rate.
3. Strategies to Mitigate Risks: Exploring methods like pre-selling and leveraging industry contacts to reduce the risks associated with reaching the breakeven point.

Key Questions for You to Seriously Answer

1. Breakeven Point Calculation: How will you calculate your breakeven point, and what are the critical variables (fixed expenses, direct costs, projected sales) involved in this calculation?
2. Cash Flow and Losses: What is your plan for managing cash flow and covering losses until your business reaches the breakeven point?
3. Funding and Resources: What sources of funding will you use to sustain your business before reaching breakeven, and how will you ensure you have enough to cover all necessary expenses?
4. Burn Rate Awareness: Have you calculated your business's burn rate, and how long can you sustain operations before running out of cash and credit?
5. Risk Mitigation Strategies: What strategies can you employ, such as pre-selling or leveraging industry contacts, to mitigate the risks associated with not reaching the breakeven point quickly?

Investors vs. Entrepreneurs

Lesson #6 Investors vs. Entrepreneurs.

You're absorbing a program about getting into business so that must make you an entrepreneur, right?

Well, maybe not.

You see, in my career, I've met lots of people who've owned businesses but not all of them were entrepreneurs.

Let me summarize for you what I see as an entrepreneur…

An entrepreneur is someone who has a dream. They see something in their mind that doesn't exist yet and then undertake the actions that they believe are necessary to make it happen. The plan may not answer all questions at the time it begins but the entrepreneur proceeds anyway, believing that the necessary pieces will fall into place when the right time comes.

Now, please notice that I did not put the word 'business' anywhere in that description.

I don't believe that entrepreneurs are limited to the world of business or that they necessarily own the organization they work in.

A salesperson in a big company can be an entrepreneur when they develop a new and different way of finding customers or delivering value.

A clergyperson can be an entrepreneur when founding a new congregation.

A mother can be an entrepreneur when she sets upon a mission to figure out how to homeschool her kids.

The mainstay of entrepreneurship is to set upon a journey that has *unknowns* in an effort to make a dream come true.

Now you can see how Walt Disney and Elon Musk fit so well into this entrepreneurship category.

So, then, what about the guy who runs the corner store at the end of the block.

Isn't he an entrepreneur?

Maybe, or maybe not.

He may be an investor.

This is someone with a very different mindset than an entrepreneur.

An investor asks themselves, 'If I put in this capital, what kind of return am I likely to generate?'

Investors don't always require a 'sure thing.'

Many will accept certain levels of risk.

This means that both investors and entrepreneurs start businesses, but usually in very different ways.

People can also change over time.

I remember the first businessperson who sat in my business brokerage office who expressed this statement-

I know what it takes to start a business. I'll never do that again!

This did not mean that they were done with business, only that they had permanently moved from being an entrepreneur to becoming an investor.

Investors want more certainty as to what can be expected from a venture before they'll commit their resources.

Investors will likely prefer to buy an existing business over starting one from scratch.

Even if they do invest in a startup business, it is likely going to be something with a more certain outcome, like opening a tried-and-true type of business in an area where market research reveals that there is sufficient demand.

This isn't also to say that entrepreneurs won't buy a business either.

Because I've got experience with that as well which we'll discuss later on.

If entrepreneurs are dreamers, then, how do they make sure they don't fail in their normal life responsibilities while chasing these fantasies?

Being a responsible adult means knowing what you need to take care of and making sure you don't fail.

That's why we're going to be talking about managing these risks in the next lesson.

Key Themes (Lessons)

1. Defining Entrepreneurs vs. Investors: Understanding the differences between entrepreneurs, who pursue dreams and take risks, and investors, who seek returns on their investments with a focus on calculated risks.
2. Mindset and Approach: Recognizing that entrepreneurs and investors have different mindsets and approaches to starting and running businesses.
3. Evolution of Roles: Acknowledging that individuals can evolve from being entrepreneurs to investors as their experiences and goals change over time.

Key Questions for You to Seriously Answer

1. Self-Identification: Do you see yourself more as an entrepreneur with a vision to create something new, or as an investor looking for a return on investment? Why?
2. Risk Tolerance: What is your level of risk tolerance? Are you comfortable with the uncertainties and potential failures that come with being an entrepreneur, or do you prefer the calculated risks of an investor?
3. Motivations and Goals: What are your primary motivations and goals for starting or acquiring a business? Are they aligned more with the entrepreneurial drive to create and innovate, or the investor's aim for financial returns?
4. Resource Commitment: How much time, effort, and resources are you willing to commit to your business venture? Do these commitments reflect the mindset of an entrepreneur or an investor?
5. Future Planning: How do you envision your role evolving over time? Do you see yourself transitioning from an entrepreneur to an investor as you gain experience and achieve certain milestones?

Hedging Entrepreneurial Risk

Lesson #7, Hedging Entrepreneurial Risk.

In our earlier lesson on resources, I discussed how someone starting a business needed to have some idea of a 'plan B' in case things don't work out.

We also discussed the need for a pivot fund in order to take care of our living expenses while implementing the Plan B.

There are many out there in the business of <u>business motivation</u> who will tell you that you just need to work hard, be dedicated and success will follow.

Some people refer to this as *entrepreneurship porn* or *success porn*.

(See Harvard Business Review article, '<u>The Dangerous Rise of "Entrepreneurship Porn'</u> January 06 ,2014)

They want to invoke a feeling in you that may not be founded on much substance.

They'll tell you that having a plan B is like inviting failure into your life.

Well, these people do not have to figure out how to pay your mortgage or rent if your business fails and we already know that the <u>vast majority</u> of new businesses don't make it.

I prefer to plan for all contingencies.

Maybe it's because I'm a Boy Scout, but I like to *be prepared*.

Let's take a moment to discuss other strategies for hedging risk when starting a business.

Firstly, what is 'hedging.'

It's a financial term related to hedgerows in landscaping.

At one time, it was popular to define the boundaries of a property by planting shrubs or hedges to make a naturally growing fence.

It marks a limit.

In the financial term, it means you're limiting your losses or risks.

So, how do we begin?

Firstly, we need to quantify our responsibilities.

Do this by making a list of all the things you have to pay for each month.

We're going to refer to this number as your monthly hurdle figure.

Think of hurdle runners in the Olympics. They must get over that barricade to keep moving forward.

You do too.

Your first goal in business is to have your business grow to the point where you can withdraw this amount each month as quickly as possible.

You won't have reached the point of success in that moment, but you will have started to cover your personal minimum subsistence level.

This doesn't sound very prosperous but believe me, when you hit this point, you'll want to celebrate.

This monthly hurdle figure is also important for figuring out your pivot reserve.

If your plan B might take two months to activate, you then need two times your monthly hurdle amount in a savings account somewhere.

Don't forget, if you plan on taking on debts to start your business, then you'll need to add these payments to your 'hurdle figure' so that you can stay current on them while running the business or you figure out what you'll be doing next in case you have to activate your pivot.

Not being able to cover your bills and service your business debts while you pivot to a plan B is a guarantee that if the business fails, you'll be declaring bankruptcy.

Now back to Plan A- the business. If you feel it will take you 3 months before you can start taking any salary from the business, then you'll need three times your hurdle amount saved to support yourself in the beginning.

In order to reduce risk overall, we need to either reduce this hurdle amount, or, have other income sources that can take on some of the burden.

For example, if you're married to a spouse with enough income to meet all your monthly obligations, then you're already done... as long as they're willing to support you.

Take a look at each of the items on your monthly responsibility list.

Are there any you can remove?

Finding ways to reduce the hurdle figure can often be easier than earning more money.

Do you need to be driving a car with a payment? Or could you sell it, pay the debt and drive something cheaper or use transit?

Are there monthly expenses you could cut?

Could you move to a cheaper place?

Could you take a part-time job in the off hours to help support yourself while you grow your business during its main operating times?

Could you start the business while you keep your job and have it already able to meet part of your monthly hurdle before you quit your job?

These are all ideas that I would challenge you to consider.

I have met many people who have made lifestyle sacrifices in order to reduce the risk of getting into business.

The other side of this coin is that reducing your monthly hurdle rate also can give a new business a greater chance of success since you can afford to leave more money in the business before drawing your minimum salary.

When I bought the business brokerage, I knew the cash flow would be turbulent.

I felt prepared though because I had several months of living expenses saved up and I owned some apartment buildings which were creating cash flow for me.

My wife at the time also had her own income and paid some of the bills at home.

The startup phase of a business and the uneasy time spent enacting a pivot are lean times that most people don't fully appreciate until they've gone through them.

If you've ever heard stories from your elders about 'hard times,' this is it.

If you only ever counted on spending what you NEED to spend to keep going, it means a lot of fun things get cut like restaurants or vacations.

I remember very distinctly during one of my business startup phases having to turn down invitations to go out and meet friends because I couldn't afford the gas, let alone any money for food or beer.

This is a thing that requires dedication and discipline.

Alternatively, you could simply buy a business that already has customers and sales and employees and pay yourself a full salary starting from your first week.

And this is why most of the people who I work with who are trying to get into a business choose to go down this acquisition path.

It's inherently less risky than starting something new. (Although if you don't do it correctly, it can be just as risky as a startup.)

Next let's talk about how one finds the money to buy a business and contrast that with starting something new.

Key Themes (Lessons)

1. Hedging Entrepreneurial Risk: Understanding the importance of planning for risks and having a contingency plan (Plan B) in case the business doesn't succeed.
2. Quantifying Responsibilities and Setting Hurdles: Identifying personal and business financial responsibilities to determine the monthly hurdle figure needed for basic survival and business operations.
3. Reducing Risk through Lifestyle Adjustments: Exploring strategies to reduce personal expenses and finding alternative income sources to lower the financial burden during the business startup phase.

Key Questions for You to Seriously Answer

1. Plan B and Pivot Fund: What is your Plan B if your business doesn't succeed, and how much money do you need to set aside in a pivot fund to cover your living expenses while you implement this plan?
2. Monthly Hurdle Figure: What are your monthly financial responsibilities, including personal and business expenses? How can you calculate your monthly hurdle figure to ensure you meet these obligations?
3. Expense Reduction: What personal expenses can you reduce or eliminate to lower your monthly hurdle figure? Consider things like car payments, housing costs, and discretionary spending.
4. Alternative Income Sources: What alternative income sources can you utilize to support yourself during the startup phase of your business? Could you keep your current job, take a part-time job, or leverage a spouse's income?
5. Preparedness and Sacrifice: Are you prepared to make the necessary sacrifices and lifestyle adjustments to reduce your financial risk? What specific steps will you take to ensure you can sustain yourself during the lean times of your business startup?

Using Debt

Lesson #8, Using debt in financing your business.

To make a business go, we sometimes need stuff or services.

This stuff and these services can oftentimes be bought with borrowed money.

Earlier in the program, I've mentioned debt a few times.

In this lesson, we're going to dig more deeply into how people get themselves in debt and the big differences between business and personal credit.

First, let me tell you a story and some facts.

When I operated my business brokerage, very few of the business buyers I worked with were able to qualify for any amount of business debt.

Less than a quarter of them to be precise.

Business debt is debt issued to a business for a business purpose.

It is normally still personally guaranteed by the business owner.

Examples of business debt might be a mortgage on a commercial or industrial building, a line of credit to help finance inventory or receivables, or a business credit card for travel or office expenses.

The borrower in these instances is a business entity.

If you live in the USA, you can even get a business loan to buy an existing business though guarantees provided by the US Small Business Administration.

For the rest of the world, business borrowing when buying a business is still largely tied to the 'stuff' that you're buying.

For example, if you're buying a business for $1,000,000 and the business contains equipment and inventories worth $500,000 and the bank agrees to lend you 75% of the value of these tangible items, then you would qualify for a bank loan of $375,000.

Why would someone pay $1,000,000 for a business with only $500,000 worth of stuff?

When you buy a business, you're not buying stuff, you're buying a cash flow, and we'll cover this in another lesson.

Now, how did many of those business buyers buy businesses if they couldn't qualify for any business financing?

They used personal debt instruments.

Personal debt is issued to people for personal consumption, spending or investment needs.

Banks make business lending decisions based on the past performance of the business they are lending to or that you're buying.

They also need to know that you understand how to run the business profitably.

Banks see businesses as risky, and they have the data to prove it... remember how most small businesses fail within a few years?

Well, this leads bankers to be very conservative when it comes to lending money to businesses.

People, on the other hand, seemingly represent a lower risk for banks because of their ability to earn employment income.

Let's get back to those 75% of business buyers who couldn't get a business loan...

Often, these people would go to a bank and ask to get a loan to buy a business.

They would get rejected for two principal reasons-

1. The bank didn't like the business for some reason.
2. The bank didn't like the applicant for some reason.

Now, some of those buyers would go back the very next day and speak to a personal loan officer instead of the small business loan agent.

They would regularly get approved for such things as credit cards, car loans, lines of credit, new mortgage financings, and more.

These borrowers would present their history of employment income and get approved by the bank.

They would then use the money to buy a business and likely quit their job.

The plan to quit their job would be a secret withheld from the banker for sure.

For most start-up entrepreneurs, it is these personal credit facilities that often have to be relied upon in order to get money to start a business.

Sometimes, countries may have small business lending programs in order to help encourage economic growth.

Many of these programs are tied to hard costs, such as acquiring machinery and equipment or fitting up a leased business location.

There can also be programs available for certain groups such as women, young adults or other disadvantaged people that may be used for start-up financing.

Where I live, for example, there is a government economic development agency that will lend young entrepreneurs under the age of 35 up to $20,000 to start a business.

Sometimes, these government agencies don't look very carefully at the deals and might also make these loans available to someone buying a small business.

I have never heard of any bank lending program, whether government guaranteed or otherwise which did not require some level of equity investment on the part of the entrepreneur.

This means that in order to borrow to get into business, one needs to already have some level of cash to inject themselves whether for paying a business seller or just covering other transaction costs.

This is often expressed as a minimum debt to equity ratio.

For example, many banks globally require a 3:1 debt to equity ratio meaning that if you have one dollar of your own to put into the business, you can borrow up to three more and perhaps only if you have collateral to support the loan as well.

Various government programs can skew this ratio depending on where you live and whether real estate is involved as banks will usually be willing to lend more against this class of assets.

So far, we've been talking about banks as lenders.

There are other sources of debt financing for your business as well.

You can use leasing companies to help provide equipment and furniture.

You can use factoring companies who will advance money to you in exchange for transferring receivables to them.

Companies like Dell Computer will often finance electronic equipment you might need just like a car manufacturer might.

But there is one class of lender that is only available to those who are buying existing businesses- the seller.

Just because a business transaction might occur on a specific day to become the new owner of an existing business, that doesn't mean the seller gets all the money that day.

In the vast majority of business sale transactions, the seller is left 'holding paper' on closing day.

There are many terms for this:

- Vendor take back financing
- Seller financing
- Holding a note
- Installment sale
- And other similar terms found around the world.

The fact is that most operating businesses are sold with this purchase formula...

1. Some money from the buyer,
2. some money from the bank if possible and
3. some money paid over time to the seller.

This seller financing is still debt, just like a bank loan, but you owe it to the person or business entity who sold you the business.

The banker, for example, will count the seller financing in their overall debt to equity calculations.

Sometimes, the bank may consider seller financing to be like equity, but usually only if there is no required payment for several years.

Basically, the seller would have to hand over the keys to their business for several years without getting payments on this outstanding debt. That can be tough to negotiate but not impossible.

It is very, very, very difficult for an 'outsider' to buy a business with no money, regardless of what you might hear from internet gurus who make money selling courses on this topic.

So, the question is, if you have some amount of money with which to get into business, why would you start something new which is unproven when you can leverage the history of a successful business for sale to get bank and seller financing?

I've discovered that there are usually three reasons people give for choosing the startup over a business acquisition:

1. They didn't think of it.
2. They don't have enough money to invest even with the financing options available.
3. They have a specific dream of what they want to create and there are no businesses like that around them.

There is a subtle difference here between seller financing and an 'earnout' or 'royalty.'

Earnouts and Royalties are based upon the buyer giving the seller an amount of money over time based on the future performance of the business, ie 'I'll pay you $100,000 for the business and then give you 4% of sales for the next 48 months.

This certainly creates a liability, but the exact amount is not defined.

If an earnout or royalty are going to be used in conjunction with a bank loan, be sure to discuss the concept with your banker as they'll likely have some input into how they look at these scenarios.

In The United States, for example, the Small Business Administration wants a defined figure in the agreement for how much is being paid for the business. So a royalty or earnout won't work in that situation. Instead, you have to work with the same concept in reverse, a seller note with provisions for debt forgiveness if the performance doesn't hit your targets.

For a real in-depth lesson on how to buy a business in a risk-controlled way, check out my online course that I've been delivering and improving since 2008 over at https://www.BusinessBuyerAdvantage.com

So then, let's say you don't have the required amount of money?

Next, we'll get into entrepreneurship for broke people...

Key Themes (Lessons)

1. Understanding Business vs. Personal Debt: Distinguishing between business debt, which is borrowed for business purposes and often personally guaranteed, and personal debt, which is borrowed for personal needs but can be used to finance a business.
2. Sources of Debt Financing: Exploring various sources of debt financing for businesses, including banks, government programs, leasing companies, factoring companies, and seller financing.

3. Strategic Use of Debt: Understanding how to strategically use debt to finance a business, including the importance of having some equity investment and considering seller financing as part of the purchase formula.

Key Questions for You to Seriously Answer

1. Debt Utilization Strategy: How do you plan to use debt to finance your business? Will you rely more on personal debt or business debt, and why?
2. Qualifying for Business Loans: Do you understand the requirements and criteria for qualifying for business loans in your area? What steps will you take to meet these criteria?
3. Debt-to-Equity Ratio: What is your target debt-to-equity ratio for financing your business? How much of your own money are you prepared to invest to secure additional financing?
4. Alternative Financing Sources: Besides traditional bank loans, what other sources of debt financing can you explore for your business? Consider leasing companies, factoring companies, and seller financing.
5. Managing Debt and Risk: How will you manage the risks associated with taking on debt to finance your business? What is your plan for ensuring you can meet debt obligations while maintaining business operations?

Creativity and Resourcefulness

Lesson #9 Being creative and resourceful when you need to be.

In my years as a business broker and private transaction advisor, I have always asked the business sellers I've worked with why they got into business.

We may imagine that there are a lot of generational businesses or people who started up because of a dream to create the perfect business but one answer surprised me at first.

Until I heard it over and over again.

'I needed to start a business, I was forced to, I didn't have a choice, I had responsibilities and needed an income.'

Yes, necessity is the mother of invention.

Many of these forced entrepreneurs came to the field of business ownership with very few resources to speak of.

Now, having little money is not necessarily a bad thing.

In fact, not having money can make for a better business.

When we have access to money it becomes easy to just spend our way out of any problems.

When that option is not there, we must be resourceful.

We must learn to ask, 'how can we solve this problem for free or for very little money?'

Luckily for you, this is the best time in history to start a business with little to no money.

Why?

Because of the disruptive aspects of the internet.

Let me give you an example...

Back in the early 90's if you wanted to accept credit cards you had to have bank accounts at different banks which were part of either the Visa or MasterCard networks.

If you wanted to accept AMEX, you had to qualify with them and sometimes they made you wait 30 days for your money.

All of this meant that it was a hassle to accept cards and some of the banks would want you to have minimum balances all the time in case of fraudulent chargebacks or claims.

In the early 2000's, I ran a business and by that time I was able to accept all credit cards and call a toll-free number where I would input all the card numbers and expiry dates and the charge amounts.

Three days later, the money would be in my account.

Nowadays, I have an app on my phone which lets me accept credit cards and the money is in my account the next day.

This means that technology has reduced the operating capital needs of businesses that get paid at the point of sale.

Literally, technology has made it cheaper to be in business.

Another example, just a few years ago any new business needed to invest in a point-of-sale system (POS) which might have cost thousands of dollars.

Today, you can get an integrated POS and payment system as a software solution which will run on a tablet for a monthly fee.

Many things that once required big investments now exist as software services or SaaS solutions as they are called. (Software as a Service.)

You can even avoid going to the post office by buying postage and printing labels on your computer.

Expensive ecommerce setups can now be done easily with solutions such as Shopify or selling on an established marketplace online like Amazon.

So, then, what is the best type of business to start for someone who has little money and needs to be profitable as soon as possible?

It usually means a service business.

Solving a problem for someone.

Why?

Because most service businesses are labor-intensive vs. being capital-intensive.

Capital-intensive means you need a lot of machinery and investment to make the business go, like manufacturing a product or even running a food-truck.

You can do a service yourself and then as you grow you can hire other people to do it and earn a premium off the difference you pay the employees vs what you charge your customers.

Remember our lesson about debt?

Labor is actually a great source of debt financing for your business since you pay your employees after they have done the work and sometimes with a delay.

For example, I know many businesses that pay employees every two weeks by paying them for week one and two at the end of week three.

Think about that, the employee waits 21 days for the money they earned on day one, 20 days for the money they earned on day two and so on.

This amounts to interest-free lending to the business and as long as you can collect from customers before you pay the employees. You can grow this business as fast as you can find new customers and workers.

Now, if your customers pay you 30 or 45 days after you provide the service, then you have a big problem because you will then have to find money to pay staff before you receive this money.

This is why you need to think a lot about the terms of credit and the flow of cash in your business.

So, if you need money now, you should be thinking about a business where you can scale with employees and you collect at the point of service or product delivery.

Earlier, I mentioned that a food-truck was an example of a capital-intensive business because the food-truck itself costs a lot of money.

Someone could start a party and event catering business, for example, and save up the down payment on a food truck and get financing for the balance.

The fact that you will have a history of profitability with a food business will give the lender comfort that you will know how to properly run the food truck.

This self-funding of growth is called 'bootstrapping.' The term comes from the expression 'pulling yourself up by the bootstraps.'

As your business grows and grows, your cash flow should grow too.

Now, let's do a little case study about resourcefulness and I'm going to lean in on some of my own experiences here and things I've seen others do.

Let's say you believe there is a need for a moving company in your area.

Moving companies have employees, trucks, and other tools of the trade to disassemble furniture and move it to a new home.

They're also burdened with some high costs for worker's compensation insurance and liability insurance in case they break something while on the job.

How could you get into the moving business without much or any money?

First, let's tackle the truck. Those are expensive.

Do you really need to own it? For example, here are some ideas:

1. Rent a truck for the day when you have a customer.
2. Find a business that has a suitable truck which is not being used all the time, maybe you could rent it on certain days.
3. Find an enclosed trailer you could rent or buy, hire a truck to move it from place to place once it's full or empty.
4. Find a mover in another city close by who has excess capacity, get a day rate from them for the truck and driver.

Now that we've hit the idea of using another mover's truck, how about another mover's workers as well?

If you could have an arrangement with a company that has excess capacity who will give you a rate for a truck and two workers, then all you have to do is figure out how to quote the jobs properly and you'll make money on each one.

Further to this- what if you want a guarantee of making money with every move?

How about you simply advertise for customers and sell the jobs, then contract the service to another company?

How about making other movers bid for the jobs?

How about making them bid for leads you generate? Now you don't even have to go quote the jobs.

Do you see where I'm heading with this?

With enough creative thinking, you can find a way to add value and maneuver the inflows and outflows of cash such that you can ensure you're making money with each job or avoid making big investments that you may not be able to afford.

Then, it's just a matter of securing enough customer inquiries to create the cash flow you need.

This is important because if you ever get tired of running your service business, you'll want to be able to sell it and hopefully for more than the value of the stuff it owns.

That's what we're going to discuss next, how to put a price on a business…

Key Themes (Lessons)

1. Necessity and Resourcefulness: Highlighting that many successful entrepreneurs start their businesses out of necessity and learn to be resourceful with limited resources.
2. Capital vs. Labor-Intensive Businesses: Emphasizing the benefits of starting service-oriented, labor-intensive businesses over capital-intensive ones, especially when funds are limited.

3. Creative Solutions and Bootstrapping: Encouraging the use of creative solutions and bootstrapping to grow a business without significant upfront investment.

Key Questions for You to Seriously Answer

1. Necessity and Motivation: Are you starting your business out of necessity? How can this drive your resourcefulness and creativity in overcoming financial limitations?
2. Type of Business: Is your business idea more capital-intensive or labor-intensive? How can you minimize initial investments and focus on scalable, labor-intensive opportunities?
3. Creative Problem-Solving: What creative solutions can you think of to reduce costs and solve problems without spending money? How can you leverage existing resources and partnerships?
4. Cash Flow Management: How will you manage the cash flow in your business to ensure you can pay employees and cover expenses while waiting for customer payments? What terms will you set to maintain a healthy cash flow?
5. Bootstrapping Strategies: What bootstrapping strategies can you implement to grow your business gradually using profits and minimal external funding? How can you reinvest earnings to scale your operations?

Valuing Businesses

Lesson #10 How do we value an operating business?

In this lesson, we're going to address two big questions: What do small businesses sell for AND the follow up question that everyone asks once they've heard the answer to question 1, who would sell a good business for that amount of money?

So, let's begin.

When someone buys a business, they've normally got two hats on, the investor hat and the job-seeker hat.

You see, most small business buyers will become the day-to-day manager of the business, so they're going to be getting a job out of this deal.

Their investor personality, however, if you want to imagine business buyers as having multiple personality disorder, wants to earn a rate of return on the money that is invested in the deal.

As you can see, neither of these two objectives can be measured or relied upon in the case of a new business startup.

Only buying an established business can give you any degree of certainty that you'll be able to earn a salary and get a return on the money you put in.

So, if a business provides enough money to cover your wages and give you a return on your investment, how much should you pay for this cash flow?

It's a great question and you'll find people all over the place who will debate this and give different answers.

The most common way of determining the value of a small business is by multiplying its discretionary cash flow.

The discretionary cash flow is the amount of cash available to an owner operator who works full time in the business. Sometimes referred to as SDE (Sellers Discretionary Earnings.)

So, in order to determine this, we need to go through a process called normalization to remove non-cash expenses from the income statement and to add back any adjustments for items of profit that have been concealed as expenses for tax management purposes.

Things like the expense for a cell phone given to the owner's daughter. This is not a real business expense and represents part of the profit of the business.

And NO, you're not really allowed to do this kind of thing but small business owners all around the world will do this kind of thing to lower their tax bill, especially in high-tax countries.

You also must be sure that you're valuing just a business. For example, if the business owns real estate, then the land and building has to be normalized out so that we're just looking at the operating business.

Real estate is evaluated in very different ways.

Now, what I'm going to share with you is for small businesses only. This means the discretionary cash flow is less than $500,000 a year generally.

Also remember, this is a super-simplified example just to give you a taste of how this works...

What we do is take the discretionary cash flow and multiply it based on the risk of the business.

For a service business with little in the way of assets or barriers preventing new competitors from starting up this multiplier could be 1.5 or 1.7. Maybe up to 2 at a stretch.

For a general resale business with inventory, it could be 2 or 2.5.

For a business with a lot of equipment and machinery, it could be as high as 3.

So, our party-catering business with $100,000 a year in discretionary cash flow is worth about $150-$170K.

For some of you this may be shocking.

But don't forget that businesses are risky as we've already mentioned several times in this program.

Business buyers are investors, they want to know what they're putting in and what the return on their time and money will be.

Also, please note that the discretionary earnings are only obtained by a full-time owner operator.

This means that in this example we're imagining, the $100,000 of cash flow is obtained by investing $150,000 and the *full-time hours* needed to operate the business.

It means that once you consider the value of your time and efforts, the return on investment is much longer than the 1.5 years we see at first glance.

A proper business valuation is done by a painstakingly accurate normalization process and then research into past transaction databases to see what similar businesses sold for in the same industry.

A restaurant with the same cash flow as a septic-pumping business will always sell for less because the restaurant industry is riskier than septic tank pumping.

There is also a need to examine the 'excess assets' of the business as this will add to the price. Often, long-time profitable businesses have a surplus of operating capital, for example, or other assets that are worth money but don't contribute to the operations.

These must be dealt with either via the seller keeping them, liquidating them separately, or making them part of the deal with the buyer.

I have done hundreds of these valuations for business owners in many countries and all of them say the same thing when I present the results...

"I could just have the same money if I kept the business for the next few years."

AND- they're absolutely correct.

This is why it never really makes sense to sell a good business. Ever.

So, who sells them then?

Those who are being pushed by a pressing personal motivation.

Business sellers generally have one of these five reasons for selling:

1. Burnout and fatigue- They simply can't endure the idea of running the business anymore. If you had a job for a long time that you didn't enjoy anymore, you'd quit once you found a new one. Business owners don't have this luxury, they need to find a buyer if the business can be sold.
2. Illness- they're sick and don't have anyone to pass the business on to.

3. Divorce- They may owe half the business' value to a spouse they're leaving and don't want to pay them out, the answer is often to sell the business so each partner can take their share.
4. Relocation- They're married, and their spouse has a more lucrative opportunity in a new city. The business must be sold so the owner can join their spouse in the new location.
5. Retirement- it's time to hit the golf course in Arizona on a daily basis.

So, as you can see, buying a business is not as expensive as you may have thought.

You can make money from it from the first day you're the new owner and it's easier to finance since you can often access seller financing and banks are more interested in financing a business with a demonstrated cash flow.

Most importantly, you won't be facing an uncertain period of financing your operating losses while you race to hit your breakeven point.

If you end up owning a business and want to learn more about the selling side, be sure to check out my resources such as books and courses at https://www.HowToSellMyOwnBusiness.com

The only challenge for you then is finding a suitable business to buy.

That's what we'll discuss in the next lesson…

Key Themes (Lessons)

1. Valuation of Small Businesses: Understanding how small businesses are valued based on their discretionary cash flow and the associated risk multipliers.
2. Investor vs. Job-Seeker Perspective: Recognizing that most small business buyers are both investors seeking a return on their investment and job seekers looking for a salary.
3. Motivations for Selling: Identifying the primary reasons business owners decide to sell their businesses, often driven by personal circumstances.

Key Questions for You to Seriously Answer

1. Valuation Understanding: How do you determine the value of a small business you are interested in buying? Are you familiar with the process of calculating discretionary cash flow and applying risk multipliers?
2. Balancing Investor and Job-Seeker Roles: How do you plan to balance the roles of being an investor and a day-to-day manager in a business? What are your expectations for both salary and return on investment?
3. Risk Assessment: What factors will you consider to assess the risk of the business you are evaluating? How will these factors influence the multiplier you apply to the discretionary cash flow?
4. Motivation for Selling: Why is the current owner selling the business? How does their reason for selling impact your evaluation of the business's potential and stability?
5. Financial and Personal Readiness: Are you financially and personally ready to purchase and operate a small business? What steps have you taken to prepare for the responsibilities and risks involved?

Finding a Business to Buy

Lesson #11, Finding a business to buy.

Where does one find a business to buy?

It depends on whether the business is *for sale* or not.

Also, there is something special about selling a small business- Owners don't want people to know it's for sale.

That's right, the market for small businesses is a secret one which makes it quite different from anything else.

We've also got two kinds of sellers, those who have their business for sale and those who don't.

If you go online and search 'businesses for sale,' you'll find several large marketplace websites where business brokers and owners are advertising various businesses.

Business brokers are professionals who help people market and sell an operating business.

They are very different from real estate agents, although in some places, business brokers are required to have real estate licenses in order to operate and this adds to confusion in an already complex marketplace.

Business brokers typically charge a commission for selling a business and the process can take quite some time.

The biggest hurdle is finding the right buyer.

Someone with the anticipated down-payment requirements and with experience in the industry such that a banker will be more likely to make a business acquisition loan.

When you go online and search the ads for businesses that are for sale, you'll see descriptions such as 'family friendly restaurant franchise for sale, cash flow $150,000/year. Asking $550,000"

That's it. No address, no name, nothing.

The seller wants it to be a secret and the only people who find out what business it is are those who complete a non-disclosure agreement and provide proof of funds in some cases.

Why is this so?

Because when people in a market find out a business is for sale, they make all kinds of assumptions about it.

Perhaps it's failing, perhaps if they buy its products the warranty won't be honoured, perhaps the business won't survive to fill the order to be delivered next year, etc.

If employees find out, maybe they'll worry about their job security and leave to work somewhere else.

Uncertainty is something people want to avoid in their commercial dealings, and this is why these things are kept secret.

Now, would it surprise you to discover that only 20% of businesses advertised for sale ever sell?

That's because there are a lot of sellers who have terrible businesses that nobody should buy, they're looking to cash out of their money-losing enterprise to salvage their own personal finances.

Or they just don't have any idea as to how to properly price a business, so they ask too much.

Or the business is built as an extension of the individual owner with no real systems or means of properly operating it without a large degree of direct owner supervision and industry-specific knowledge. This kind of business can only be purchased by someone who is as expert in the industry as the seller!

It is perfectly normal for me to look at businesses for sale with my clients and determine that they are overpriced by two or three times. This is not a misprint.

Also, of all the businesses that are sold, only one in five are advertised for sale.

What does this mean?

It means that 80% of business owners who want to sell find someone to buy their business before they advertise it online or engage with a business broker.

Remember, we're talking about good and profitable businesses here.

Really poor performers tend to simply close.

Most owners of money-losing businesses realize that it would be hard to find anyone to pay money to assume their position.

This reality of the market means that there is more opportunity for a business buyer among businesses that are not 'for sale' rather than trying to compete with other buyers for those listed online.

The good businesses that are listed in online marketplaces will attract many buyers and therefore create competition which bids up price.

This is exactly what the sellers want, however, it costs money to pay the broker and there is always a risk that the business will become known publicly as being for sale.

Therefore, it's tempting for owners who decide to sell to find someone privately. They save a commission and take fewer perceived risks with confidentiality.

If you're serious about finding the right business to buy, you will have to undertake a networking and marketing campaign of your own to find and meet these owners before they take steps to put the business on the market.

If you need help, you may want to look at joining my online group coaching program called *Business Buyer Advantage: Group Coaching*. It's made up of people who are searching for these businesses right now and want to learn directly from me and via observing other members progress through their deals. You can learn more about the group and my other buyer services at https://www.BusinessBuyerAdvantage.com

Now, what if you can't find just the right business for sale to satisfy your creative juices?

That's what we're going to be covering in the next lesson.

Key Themes (Lessons)

1. Finding Businesses for Sale: Exploring where to find businesses for sale, including online marketplaces and through business brokers, while understanding the secretive nature of business sales.

2. Challenges in Business Acquisition: Recognizing the difficulties in finding and evaluating businesses for sale, including overpriced listings and businesses that are heavily dependent on the owner's specific skills.
3. Private Business Sales: Understanding that many businesses are sold privately before being listed publicly, emphasizing the importance of networking and proactive search strategies.

Key Questions for You to Seriously Answer

1. Searching for Businesses: Where will you start your search for a business to buy? Are you prepared to explore both public listings and private opportunities?
2. Evaluation Criteria: What criteria will you use to evaluate whether a business is worth buying? How will you determine if the asking price is fair and the business is viable?
3. Networking and Confidentiality: How will you approach networking to find businesses that are not publicly listed for sale? What strategies will you use to maintain confidentiality and build trust with potential sellers?
4. Understanding the Market: Do you understand the market dynamics, including why some businesses are overpriced or why certain businesses never make it to public listings? How will this knowledge impact your search and negotiation strategies?
5. Preparation and Resources: Are you prepared with the necessary resources, both financial and advisory, to navigate the business acquisition process? How will you ensure you have the support and knowledge needed to make a successful purchase?

Buying a Platform Business to Launch your Idea

Lesson #12 Building a new business on top of an old one.

Back in 2019, I published a book called *Smarter than a Startup*. (Available from Amazon world-wide in Kindle and audio)

The ideas in the book were earth-shattering for some who chose to read it.

So often, we exist within a certain set of ideas, and we fail to even see the assumptions we've made that frame our thinking.

One of the biggest lessons I've learned from my career in entrepreneurship is that there are no rules.

The only limits that hold you back are in your mind.

For many of you, you probably thought that buying a business was something that you could never do.

There is a lot of talk and books published on the topic of starting businesses but very little on the idea of buying them.

For most people that I work with the progression in thinking goes like this.

First, they want to start a business, but if they have a lot of personal responsibilities, the risk factors give them pause. Often, these people will have ideas about what kind of business they wish to own one day.

Then, they might stumble upon the idea of buying an already successful business and see this as less-risky but often what they see presented doesn't fit their dream.

I'm going to let you know that you can have it all.

Here's the solution, you buy a profitable business which has some or all the resources that you would need for the business you planned to start.

From day one, you continue to operate the business as the former owner did. This gives you the secure cash flow you can rely on.

Then, you start working on your startup idea and take advantage of the resources of the business.

You can now build your startup with very little additional investment while you already enjoy a cash flow from the existing business which keeps you personally solvent.

You can even use this same trick over and over to grow your business.

For example, if you want to expand to new cities, simply buy a business in the right industry and convert it over to your branding.

This is called building on a platform or 'doing a roll-up.' You find a suitable business that acts as a base of operations and then build new business offerings or brands upon it and add more similar businesses and locations and streamline the overheads by centralizing certain functions.

Let's look at a case study.

There is a local pizzeria here in my hometown.

They're like a lot of pizza joints all around the world. They do takeout, delivery and have a dining room.

Like most pizzerias, they serve lunch and supper and are open late on weekends. Not much goes on there in the morning.

So, several years ago, the owner invested in a bigger walk-in freezer because he had an idea.

He began making a frozen version of his personal sized lasagna and tried selling it as an add on for takeout orders from a small display freezer at the front cash and in local grocery stores.

The idea worked and now frozen lasagna makes up a significant portion of his sales.

He entered the frozen food business with hardly any additional investment.

Just ingredients, labour and some extra freezer space.

Second case study… the caterer at the farmer's market.

Another food business in my hometown is an event caterer.

They operate a commercial kitchen and have some specially outfitted vehicles for delivering hot food and dishware to events such as weddings and meetings.

One day while browsing a local farmer's market I found that they had a stall set up selling frozen soups.

There were several varieties all packaged in small single-serving containers.

How expensive would it be to enter this kind of business if you already had the kitchen available to you?

I'm sure your mind is spinning with ideas right now.

You are only limited by your imagination.

Just think of a business you'd like to run and ask yourself, what other kind of business would have most of the resources already in place to start this new enterprise?

But buying a business is not without risks and we'll dig deeper into that in the next section.

Key Themes (Lessons)

1. Combining Business Acquisition with Startup Ideas: Exploring the concept of buying an existing business to provide a stable cash flow and resources, which can then be used to launch new business ideas.
2. Platform Business Strategy: Utilizing a profitable existing business as a platform to build and expand new business ventures with minimal additional investment.
3. Creative Business Expansion: Demonstrating through case studies how existing businesses can diversify and expand their offerings by leveraging their current resources and infrastructure.

Key Questions for You to Seriously Answer

1. Combining Acquisition and Startup: What existing business could provide cash flow and resources to support your startup idea? How would you integrate your startup plans with the existing operations?
2. Platform Business Potential: Can you identify businesses in your desired industry that could serve as a platform for expansion? What resources or infrastructure do these businesses already have that you can leverage?
3. Creative Diversification: What additional products or services could you introduce using the existing resources of the business you acquire? How can you test these ideas with minimal investment?
4. Risk Management: What are the potential risks of buying an existing business and using it as a platform for your startup idea? How will you mitigate these risks while ensuring both the existing business and the new venture thrive?

The Biggest Risk in Buying a Small Business

Lesson #13 Don't let the existence of customers blind you to this problem.

If you've been paying close attention to my words, you'll know that I've said the following about buying a small business:

1. It is less risky than starting a new business because you already have customers and sales.
2. That many small businesses can be far overpriced.

This creates a scenario for a different kind of risk.

You see, the business a seller might sell to you is rarely the same as the business you end up buying.

A seller might be enjoying a business that delivers a cash flow (SDE) of $250,000 to them as the owner/operator.

Let's say you pay a high price for this cash flow, three times SDE, which would be a purchase price of $750,000.

Let's also say that you live in the USA, and you buy the business with a 90% Small Business Administration loan, and you do this in 2024 when interest rates are 11.5% on these loans.

This would give you a loan of $675,000 over 10 years with a monthly payment of $9,490.19. That would add up to $113,882.28 per year.

That's 45% of your discretionary cash flow of $250,000.

It is highly unlikely that the seller has such a debt that they are paying. So, they see their business as a successful little cash-printing machine. But once it gets into your hands, the cash flow suddenly becomes much skinnier because of debt service.

Let's then look at what you need to pay out of the remaining $136,118 each year:

1. You need to take a salary for your full-time efforts.
2. You need to pay any income taxes on the profits you're earning including the principal portion of that loan payment (yes, only the interest is an expense for tax purposes)
3. You need to cover the cost of any equipment purchases. (remember, we added back depreciation when calculating SDE and this is how equipment wearing out is measured)
4. You should get a return on the cash you put in as a down-payment on this highly risky asset.

As you can see, it's going to be tough to cover all these things when you've paid such a high price for this small business.

But you know what?

Many people who get excited about the idea of buying a small business will do just this kind of deal and in doing so, trade one kind of risk for another.

They'll exchange customer and sales risk for *financing risk.*

In the scenario I've just described, the business is now in a precarious position.

If we assume that the SDE of the business is 20% of revenues, this means that the business has top-line sales of $1,250,000. What if there is a 5% decline in sales next year?

It could mean you have to stop taking a paycheque out of the business.

That's seriously scary stuff.

<u>You cannot overpay for a small business.</u>

So, even though it might appear to be less risky than starting one, I always recommend you compare the two.

Recently, I had a conversation with a prospective business buyer who wanted to buy a lawn maintenance company with 120 residential clients and 7 commercial accounts.

The business had revenues of $381,000 and an SDE of $184,000.

The seller wanted $445,000 for the business, or about 2.4X SDE.

This might seem reasonable on the surface for anyone who hears that small businesses sell for 2-3X their cash flows, however, let's ask ourselves this question...

What if we invested in paying two workers to mow lawns and spent our time going door-to-door trying to recruit customers?

Do you think we could find 120 homes and 7 businesses to be our customers over a 2-year period?

Do you think we could do this for a lot less than $445,000?

Of course we could.

At the end of my conversation with the buyer, we concluded that this was a small service business with few barriers to entry.

There was little investment in equipment.

Its true value was far lower than 2.4X SDE.

Paying any more than ~$250,000 for this $184,000 cash flow didn't make sense and this represents a value of 1.35X SDE.

Or another format that might make sense would be an offer like 'I'll buy your trucks and equipment and then pay you 10% of whatever I bill these clients you'll be handing over for the next four years.'

In this kind of deal, we're essentially treating the business seller like a salesperson.

We're giving them an interest in the future performance of these client relationships.

You could call this a commission or royalty-style offer.

This kind of purchase is essentially risk-free for the buyer and is the kind of resourceful deal-making that can really set you apart.

Don't get caught up in the hype of business acquisition content that you might find online.

There is plenty of 'business success porn' in this area as well and it can infect your thinking and cause you to excitedly do something dumb.

Operating a small business is hard work and full of challenges.

Just because the owner shows a certain level of cash flow in their business doesn't mean it's guaranteed in any way to continue under your stewardship.

Yes. David is available for live events. Details at the end of this book.

Key Themes (Lessons)

1. Real Costs of Business Acquisition: Understanding how the costs of acquiring a business, especially through financing, can significantly impact cash flow and profitability.
2. Evaluating Business Value Accurately: Recognizing the importance of accurately valuing a business and considering whether starting a new business might be more cost-effective than overpaying for an existing one.
3. Mitigating Acquisition Risks: Learning strategies to minimize risks when buying a business, such as structuring deals creatively to align seller interests with future business performance.

Key Questions for You to Seriously Answer

1. Real Costs of Acquisition: Have you calculated the full costs of acquiring a business, including loan payments and necessary expenses? How will these costs impact your cash flow and profitability?
2. Accurate Valuation: How will you determine if the asking price for a business is fair? Are you considering the potential to start a similar business at a lower cost?
3. Risk Management: What strategies will you use to mitigate the risks of overpaying for a business? Can you structure the deal to tie the seller's compensation to future performance?
4. Due Diligence: What steps will you take to ensure thorough due diligence before purchasing a business? How will you verify the business's current and projected cash flow?
5. Sustainability: How will you ensure that the business you acquire will continue to generate the same cash flow under your management? What plans do you have to address potential declines in sales or revenue?

Conclusion

I'm glad you chose to spend some time with me thinking about small businesses and working on your entrepreneurship muscles.

There is no doubt in my mind that the path to freeing your time and increasing your earning potential is through business ownership.

There is no other way to directly leverage the efforts of others to increase cash flow for yourself.

If you compare owning a business to owning apartment buildings, for example, it would be hard to be able to raise profits on an apartment block by 30, 40, 50 or 100% in one year, but this kind of growth can be achieved with a business if you avoid all landmines.

Alternatively, you can also completely destroy the value of the business in one year, and this is pretty hard to do with an apartment building.

Business is not without risks, as we've studied, but there is little we are able to do in this life that is risk-free.

I love this stuff. My whole life has been spent building and operating businesses and working in jobs that improved my skills when I was between entrepreneurial fits of excitement.

Over the last fourteen years, I have spent my time in the small business buying and selling space helping people just like you.

The most tragic thing that I see is when someone gambles their future on a dream which they are convinced is a sure-fire winner.

In my experience, there is no way to know which businesses will work and which will not. Only adoption by customers in the market -AND- successful execution on the back end by competent and well-led team members will give you a chance of success.

In my business today, I help people from around the world who are interested in buying, selling, financing, managing or improving small and medium-sized businesses.

I maintain a YouTube channel with hundreds of videos on these topics that are free for you to enjoy at https://www.SmallBusinessAndDealMakingPodcast.com

You can always find me online at my blog site, www.DavidCBarnett.com and I would hope that you would take advantage of some of the additional information I have to share before gambling your time, energy, emotions and money on doing a deal that may not be as good as it appears. Be sure to join my email list while you're there.

AND- if you want to do a bit of a favour for other prospective entrepreneurs out there who are looking for realistic and pragmatic

advice about getting into business, please take a moment to leave an honest rating and review of this book.

On Kindle, you'll be prompted to leave a review at the end. If you're listening on Audible, hit the three little dots on the top right of the screen and you'll see a place to rate and review. You can also leave feedback on the Amazon purchase page.

If you downloaded the PDF from Gumroad, just look at the top left of the page where you can see the download files and there is a spot for you to leave stars and a review.

This small donation of your time can help someone just like you find information that might save them from a financial disaster.

Cheers and Best of Luck

David C Barnett

Additional Works by the Author

Other Books, Online Courses and Information about my coaching programs.

David C Barnett Product Map

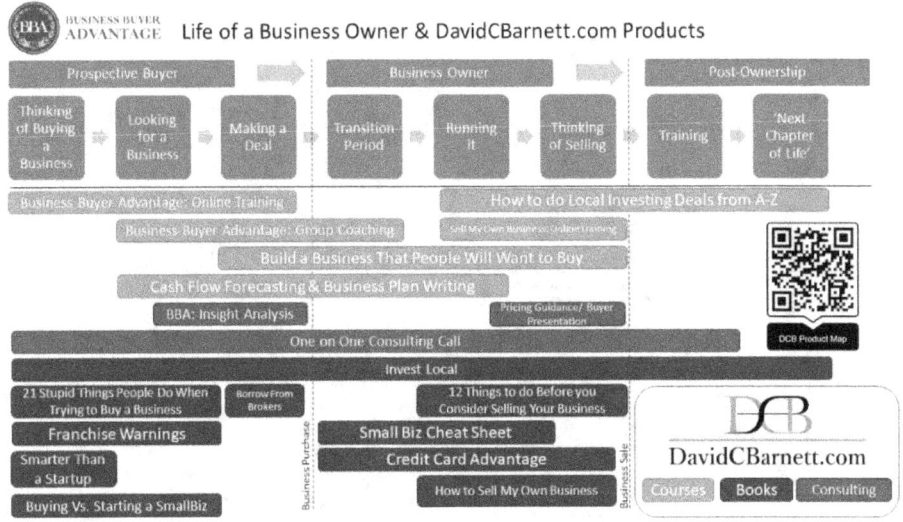

21 Stupid Things People do When Trying to Buy a Business.

Get your PDF copy from https://www.DavidCBarnett.com or Amazon Stores Worldwide for Kindle or Audio.

Want to break free of the shackles of corporate life? Want to control your own destiny and set your own hours, priorities and life direction? Simple, become an entrepreneur and start a business!

What? You don't like the risk of starting and want to buy a successful business instead? Ok, just don't do these stupid mistakes that I see novice business buyers make over and over and over again.

Every day, thousands of really awful businesses go up for sale and thousands of good businesses go up for sale with outrageously inflated asking prices.

Many of these businesses will sell to people who simply have no idea what they're getting into and don't know how to get the right guidance or advice.

Invest some time and learn from the mistakes that I've observed through my years as a business broker and private sale transaction adviser.

You really can learn from other peoples' mistakes and make yourself a better deal…. Or know when to go home and leave your money in the bank.

Now also available as an audio book from Amazon or Audible.com!

Smarter Than a Startup

Get your PDF copy from https://www.DavidCBarnett.com or Amazon Stores Worldwide for Kindle or Audio.

You've seen the hype, the raging videos from high-octane YouTubers, the dream, the lifestyle… The Startup experience.

Is it for everyone? I don't know. Does quitting your job and gambling that you'll be able to start a new business and build the clientele to the point of profitability before you run out of savings sound like a smart idea?

What about the mortgage or the kids education fund? What about feeding the kids?

A startup is a risky thing but there is a better way.

3-time best-selling author David C Barnett uses his decades of business ownership, management and consulting experience to show you the lower-risk path to owning the business of your dreams. It's not new. It may be less exciting. But your kids will get fed every day with this plan.

https://www.BusinessBuyerAdvantage.com

This is the online version of the full day seminar that I've been teaching since 2009. Learn why it makes sense to buy a business over starting one.

It has now expanded to include dozens of hours of video and audio content.

Learn how to find good businesses for sale and how to evaluate and make offers on them. How do you finance the purchase of a small business? I'll show you.

Throughout the course we use a case study and take the example step-by-step through the entire process.

If you're thinking about buying a small business to provide for your family, invest some time and money with this course before you invest hundreds of thousands of dollars in what may turn out to be a costly mistake!

Once students have completed the training in this course, they can work with me one-on-one to prepare to buy a business or join my group coaching program at https://www.BusinessBuyerAdventure.com

Since publishing, this course has been expanded to include topics such as buying distressed businesses, dealing with the Covid-19 recession, conducting share purchases, changing multipliers with larger transactions, and a deep dive into due-diligence.

Join hundreds of students just like you who want to buy a business in a risk-controlled way.

Be sure to see the comments and ratings left by our program Alumni.

https://www.BusinessBuyerAdventure.com

Visit the website for a complete tour of what's offered inside this business buyer community.

We meet several times each month to review the deals and searches of members.

Guest speakers join us each month with details on issues related to deal making or small business operations.

Members connect and network with each other in our FaceBook community.

Three levels of membership available, some with regular private one-on-one calls with David.

Access to valuation databases and company lists for Canada and USA to help in your search.

Quarterly and Annual memberships available.

All meetings since 2018 are recorded and available for you in the archive. Listen in as members discuss the real-life negotiations that happen between buyers and sellers. Sometimes, for over a year.

Help is available to help you analyze and create offers for small businesses that you find in your own search.

Choose from either a complete consulting engagement, a Buyer Insight Analysis, or ad hoc coaching/consulting calls.

Watch a video of what's included by visiting https://www.BusinessBuyerAdvantage.com

Scroll to the bottom, Step 4: Insight Analysis and Guidance.

Learn more by emailing info@alpatlantic.com or book an ad-hoc consulting call at https://www.CallDavidBarnett.com

Franchise Warnings

Get your PDF copy from https://www.DavidCBarnett.com or Amazon Stores Worldwide in paperback, audio and Kindle versions.

Franchise Warnings is the Amazon Best-Seller that tells stories that others won't.

I spent several years as a business broker and re-sold many established franchise locations. I've given advice to franchisors, helped existing franchisees sell their business and helped people buy new franchise locations.

There is a myth in the world that buying a franchise is the easy way to business success. This is far from the truth.

In this book I share what I've learned over the years. These are the stories of real people and real experiences.

The book is called Franchise Warnings because it is filled with information that you need to know before you invest your money into a franchise business.

Invest Local

Get your PDF copy from https://www.DavidCBarnett.com or Amazon Stores Worldwide in paperback, audio and Kindle versions.

Invest Local is a peek into the experience of local deal-making expert David Barnett.

His experience and education in business brokerage, small business financing and private finance deals gives him an insight into what's wrong with the common financial planning advice available today and how you can make higher investment returns while reducing risk and helping your local community.

Barnett offers step-by-step guidance on how to earn returns ranging from 9% to infinity by doing car leases, secured loans, inventory financing, buying accounts receivables, financing mini and mobile homes, operating leases on machinery and more.

High yield investing does not have to mean high-risk investing.

www.SellMyOwnBusinessSystem.com

The system is a 5-Stage process of products and services that entrepreneurs can use to exit their business on their own with help.

Visit https://www.SellMyOwnBusinessSystem.com to watch videos describing each stage.

5-Step Sell My Own Business System

1. Online Training
2. Pricing Guidance
3. Buyer Readiness
4. Buyer Selection
5. Closing

How to Sell Your Own Business

Get your PDF copy from https://www.HowToSellMyOwnBusiness.com or Amazon Stores Worldwide in paperback, audio and Kindle versions.

GET INSIDER SECRETS on how to sell your own business.

For years David C Barnett met with business owners and showed them that he could get them the maximum value for their business, now he shares these secrets with you.

When it comes time to retire, divest or simply move on to something else and you want to sell your business; read this book. You'll learn:

- When you should use a qualified business broker and when you should not
- How to sort the qualified brokers from the charlatans
- How the process should work
- What you should pay for a good broker's services
- What telltale signs to avoid
- What if you decide to sell it yourself? You'll learn:
- The process of 'For Sale by Owner' private business sales
- How to properly impress a buyer
- How not to scare off a buyer with rookie DIY mistakes
- How to find the right help for certain specific tasks that brokers usually do for their clients

In the end, if you want to do the work, you too can sell your own business and save paying a broker's commission. This book forms part of the educational tools I've prepared to help you get started in the *Sell My Own Business System*.

12 Things to do Before you Consider Selling Your Business.

Get your FREE PDF copy at https://www.HowToSellMyOwnBusiness.com or Amazon Stores Worldwide for Kindle or Audio.

Do you own a business? Do you plan to one day? Do you ever think you may want to sell that business?

I've spent years working as a business broker and consultant to buyers and sellers.

It always frustrates me when sellers show up with problems in their businesses that could easily have been solved if they had sought some advice in the years leading up to the sale.

This guide is a simple overview of the things you can do and the things you need to learn before you can successfully begin the process of selling your business for what it could truly be worth.

Now also available as an audio book from Amazon or Audible.com!

This guide forms part of the educational tools I've prepared to help you get started in the *Sell My Own Business System*.

Sell My Own Business: Online Training

https://www.HowToGetOutOfMyBusiness.com

Not sure if your business can be sold? Need a better understanding of what buyers are looking for?

What are the alternatives to selling?

Is there a better plan for your business?

What should you do in the years leading up to a potential sale?

What if you need a guaranteed schedule for exiting your business that is not guaranteed in a selling situation?

What is an Exit Plan and do you really need one?

If these questions cross your mind or if you want to learn more about how to get your business into shape to meet your exit needs, take this online course in the comfort of your home or office.

I've been doing it live since 2014 and always to overwhelmingly positive student reviews.

This half-day of online training forms part of Stage 1 of the *Sell My Own Business System*.

Build a Business That People Will Want to Buy.

www.EasySmallBizSystems.com

An easy 13-step process to get organization and systems into your small business without the need to hire expensive consultants or invest a lot of time.

Back in 2005 I started a business doing junk removal. I sold it 18 months later and the buyer admitted that the biggest reason he wanted to own it was to adapt my business systems into his other companies.

Amazing.

Business systems make companies easier to run and more profitable... meaning more valuable and desirable.

Make your life as an entrepreneur easier and more rewarding by implementing my 13-step process to build systems and a road map to getting the business and life you desire.

I promise it is easy and doesn't take much work.

I've taken clients through this process myself and none are looking back. In fact, they look forward to more vacation, higher sales, increased profits and happier employees who are empowered to shoulder their clearly-defined responsibilities.

Take the first step to building a business that people will want to buy. Enroll today.

How does an online course work? There are video modules you watch or can download as MP3 files to listen to. You work through the modules and follow along in a workbook. Supplemental files such as spreadsheets, slide presentations, Word documents and .pdf files accompany some of the modules. All the tools are provided for you to follow along and implement this process in your own business. If you need further help, I'm available to coach you through the process.

Financial Forecasting and Business Plan Writing Program

https://www.BizPlanSchool.com

Sit with David as he takes you through a 12-week course on how to design and create a cash flow forecast for either a new business or a potential acquisition target.

Learn about lead conversions, cost of goods sold, direct costs vs. overhead expenses.

Learn how to plan for the difference between 'book performance' and 'cash flow.'

Learn how the story of the profit and loss statement translates into the 'snapshot' shown in the balance sheet over time... and why this is so important to the bankers who might finance your deal.

Learn how to use your newly created cash flow forecast to make changes to your business model and magnify your chances of success.

When you're ready, you'll see how David takes the numbers and presents them in the business plan.

Whether you're courting investors or trying to get a loan officer to yell - "APPROVED," every businessperson needs to understand and develop the skills taught in this program.

What expert students say...

I have a bachelor's in finance and a Master's in Business Administration. Worked as a commercial credit analyst writing financing reports for a bank and investment analysis for many years. I can say your cash flow forecasting and business plan writing course has been one of the best training programs I've ever seen for that subject. It is very clean, well broken out, well-described, with the bonus of learning Microsoft Excel throughout the training. I was surprised how much I learned that I had never known before.
-Cody from OK

Order my Books

How to Borrow Money from your Business Broker:

A Guide to finding some of the money you need when you buy a business.

Get your PDF copy with audio and Video tutorials from https://www.DavidCBarnett.com

The book by itself is available from Amazon Stores Worldwide in audio and Kindle versions.

Business Buyers- Do you know a source of financing that can help you close the gap on financing your deal that can lend you money even if they're broke?

Yup, the business broker doing the deal.

Business Brokers- Do you worry that a seller may not want to pay you your commission or that a deal might fall apart because a buyer and seller can't agree on a price?

Are you afraid that you'll be asked to cut your commission to help the deal come together?

This book outlines a strategy that Barnett applied several times throughout his career that works for buyers and brokers in getting deals done.

Especially in tough financing environments.

ENROLL TODAY
Learn at your own pace via Video or Audio

• • •

Learn my system for analyzing, executing and leveraging local investing opportunities

www.LocalInvestingCourse.com

This online course takes you step-by-step through the same process that I use to find, underwrite and execute local investing deals. It includes over 2.5 hours of video tutorials, checklists, processes and the very notes and contracts that I use for my deals that you can use for yours.

A PDF of the Amazon Best-Seller Invest Local is included!

FREE

How to Find Local Investing Deals is the FREE audio companion to Invest Local.

Visit https://www.DavidCBarnett.com and download it today.

The recording discusses how to get out and find your first deal which will lead to referrals and is the start you need to build your own portfolio of high-yielding local investments.

Look under the FREE tab on the blog site.

Credit Card Advantage

Get your PDF copy from http://www.DavidCBarnett.com or Amazon Stores Worldwide for Kindle or Audio.

Credit Card Advantage will show you how the correct use of credit cards as a payment tool can help you achieve strategic goals in your business.

I walk readers through the step-by-step process of analyzing vendors, selecting a card program, and calculating the financial and reward benefits.

Every business owner should be using these techniques to enhance lifestyle, reduce expenses, grow sales and save on bank interest.

15 Business Finance Articles

© 2007, 2008, 2014 by David Barnett

As published in:

eNBusiness
New Brunswick's Business News

FREE
15 Business Finance Articles

Back in 2006 Barnett opened a commercial debt brokerage business.

He was a broker of commercial mortgages, business loans, factoring facilities and all types of equipment leases.

One of the ways that Barnett used to drive clients to the business was to focus on education.

In 2007, he began writing a regular monthly column for eNBusiness magazine which was published by Transcontinental Media. The publication, and the column, lasted for 2 years.

The articles have been sorted and those which remain relevant today have been put into this collection.

Please enjoy these articles and learn a little about some of the creativity and problem-solving that goes into getting the money to help a business flourish.

15 Business finance Articles is available for FREE as a PDF download by visiting http://www.DavidCBarnett.com .

Live Workshops and Seminars

2023 SMB Social Toronto sponsored by BuyAndSellABusiness.com and TD Bank.

You want your small business audience to learn something new, be exposed to impactful ideas, walk away with a plan to improve their business, and leave positive feedback about your event.

David C. Barnett is part of the formula for your success.

2023 Amherst, NS sponsored by CBDC Cumberland.

For Whom? About What?

All workshops are custom tailored to the organization and audience being served and vary in length from 45 minutes to a full day of training.

David's audiences are:

- Prospective business buyers considering entrepreneurship via acquisition.
- Owners who want to learn about selling or exiting their business.
- Owners who want to improve their business and add to its value.
- Business owners who wish to grow via acquisition.
- Economic development officers, bankers, and credit union loan officers.

The organizations who hire David are typically:

- Businesses who sell to small business owners.
- Business brokerages, law and accounting firms, financial planners and other professional firms.
- Economic development agencies.
- Business associations.
- Franchise system operators.
- Mastermind groups.

The topics that may be covered include:

- Buying businesses.
- Selling businesses.
- Financing businesses.
- Deal making.
- Business valuation.
- Business brokerage.
- Positioning a small business for sale.
- Systems and organization in small business.

Workshop Formats

-Person Live Events:

We're all looking to get back out and meet people since the pandemic years. Your prospective event attendees are no different. Ask us about what has worked in the past for other events.

These workshops make a great addition to a conference or other larger event or can be a stand-alone production intended to draw the right entrepreneurial audience.

LIVE Online Events:

Online events can be great if your audience is distributed over a large geography. They can take place in two formats; *Zoom Meetings* or *Webinars*.

Zoom Meetings allow for easy interaction amongst the attendees and is preferred for Mastermind groups or when the audience is intentionally kept small.

Webinars allow for David and a facilitator or two to be seen during a presentation, but the audience is hidden. These events can be scaled to much larger audiences and their participation is limited to asking questions or chatting in a concurrent online forum.

The facilitator is often <u>one of your</u> team members.

The Webinar format has proven very popular for events in which attendees may wish to remain anonymous with each other, such as entrepreneurs thinking about selling their business.

Post-Event Licensing and Recorded Replay:

Pricing for any live or online event is partially based on attendance.

Organizers can further extend the value of their presentation by making it available after the event has occurred regardless of whether it was a live or online event.

If this is an important feature to you, ask about having your session available post-presentation.

Learn More

Contact David C Barnett and his team to learn more about arranging your live event or to review our most recent workshop catalogue.

We can also provide references and recordings of past events to help you make a decision about whether David is the right speaker for your audience.

David's books are also available for use as attendee gifts or promotional items.

David's online platforms and social media presence can also be incorporated into a speaking arrangement to help promote your event.

Let's get together and discuss your event today.

Event Booking Line: (506) 805-3390

E-mail: BookDavid@alpatlantic.com

2023 Charlottetown, Prince Edward Island, Sponsored by CBDC Central PEI.

www.ingramcontent.com/pod-product-compliance
Lightning Source LLC
Chambersburg PA
CBHW071833210526
45479CB00001B/123